Knowing M

Bob Horne

Caterpillar Poetry

Published 2016 by
Caterpillar Poetry
simonzonenblickcaterpillarpoet.blogspot.co.uk

ISBN 978-0-9575040-2-8

Designed and typeset in Garamond by Malcolm Heron

Printed by Simprint, 30-32 Westgate, Halifax, HX1 1PW
www.simprints.co.uk

The Cricketers at Keswick was first published in *A Breathless Hush*, edited by David Rayvern Allen (Methuen, 2004); also in *Jack's Yak* by Keith Richardson (River Greta Writer, 2011).

Contents

for Samuel Horn (c.1791-1863)
agricultural labourer
and for
his ancestors and descendants

Exposure

*(W.A. Poucher, aged 89, photographs
the Wasdale Screes)*

It is evening. I have waited an hour,
walking to the shore and back a dozen times.
I like the sound of my brogues on the bright pebbles,
the give of the turf as I return to my tripod.
Cloud is building in the north.
Sometimes I am troubled by this loitering for light;
days are easily wasted.

I think of Haskett Smith, *Father of English Climbing*,
striding across early frost on Wasdale fields,
pushing through bracken as it brushes his plus-fours.
He is going to solo the first ascent of Napes Needle.
While others scrambled in gullies, he weighed up each pitch
till hand and body followed the eye
from hold to hold,
fingers firm in untouched cracks,
half-inch segs scoring the Greenstone.

Patience is *my* art.
I select, compose and frame.
The water is almost still.
Burnt umbers of autumn's fading fronds
will blur on its surface.
Boulders flock like sheep over shifting screes.
Soon, with luck, sunlight will slant along the lake.
I am ready, lens focused at infinity.

Opening

Two hands slid round the smooth wood
of the loose doorknob in front of my face.
Without help, it wouldn't budge for years.

Sometimes, across the room, I heard its double clunk,
descending chords leading to voices and footfalls,
like startled blackbirds along the unmade street;
turned to see frocks and coats as they came and went.

Or, standing by the scullery on early mornings
felt the fresh, cold air, saw from the living-room light
the back yard's broken flags, a bank of vetch
beneath the rough-topped wall, with a gap
where a gate might have been.

Then, across, a terraced row of blackened sandstone;
above its slates stars, and darkness
beginning to thin.

Living Room

I remember winter mornings
in nineteen fifty-one,
standing on the corner
of a ragged hearth-rug,
austere light from outside
screened by clothes on the creel.

With a hand-brush's worn bristles
he swept cold ashes
from under the grate,
shovelled them onto paper
to be parcelled and stuffed
in the dustbin.

Then, a scratch,
and a bud of flame
felt along the ends
of knots of newsprint.
As they browned and flaked,
fire flowed through a stack

of sticks and coal from the cellar,
a rush of smoke
slid up the sooty
blackness of the chimney
to vanish in faraway air.

I turned to look across the room,
the heat at my back.
Still, in the middle
of a flickering wall,
my grown-up shadow
gazed back at me.

Raw Material

In the donkey field
at the far end of our street
over by the railway
was an underground stream.

There never was a donkey;
only cows, or nothing
but us, climbing thorn trees,
lighting fires from dry grass

with a magnifying glass
and the sun, dead twigs
cracking, sparking beneath
a circle of still heads

and crouched bodies, blue flame
fighting for the moment
when one of us could blow it
gently into itself.

After heavy rain we ran
from our terraced homes
across soggy tussocks
to see the stream bed shiver

with miraculous liquidity,
cupped its clearness,
threw it at the air,
laughed at its scattering,

dammed the flow
with stones and mud
so that its water swelled,
danced in its new depth.

Then, one day, an end of it.
They came to build houses.
Diggers scored a deep trench.
Workmen laid the drains.

Raft

That summer I was strong enough
to swim out, haul myself from the water
on to the black wooden boards
as the tide smacked at its sides.

From harbour to headland
chalk cliff to shoreline
summer colour covered the sands,
spilled into the fringes of the sea.

I turned my back on the shallows
busy with the clamour of paddlers,
swayed on the ups and downs of waves
reeling in through grey-green emptiness,

balanced on the raft, still not adrift
but out of my depth, loving it.

Rock Pool

Once I wandered to the edge of the bay
past kite-flyers, sandcastles, beach cricket,

picked a steady path across seaweed and sharp rocks
to crouch over life the tide had left behind:

necklaces of mussels, a starfish skulking in the shingle,
clinches of limpets, too fast for small fingers to shift,

before black waves buried the world,
bundled land back to the cliff

and intertidal creatures took their chances
beneath the dark heave of sea.

Next day my pool came again.
No trace of starfish, perhaps a crab

scuttling sideways over pebbles big as boulders,
empty blue-black shells but still, with a significance

beyond my understanding, single-minded limpets
clinging to their piece of planet.

Great Leap Forward

The salt in a packet of potato crisps
used to come in a blue greaseproof sachet
contained inside the packet.
Open the sachet,
sprinkle the crystals,
and shake.

Achieving uniformity was problematic:
those at or near the bottom
were frequently deprived of seasoning
while those at the top
benefited from an excess.

I remember my first ready-salted crisp.
We were playing cricket in the park
when Nipper Norris came round the wall
at the corner of Ackroyd's garden,
stood at deep square leg and shouted
You lot, look what I've got!

This would have been about the time
of the first Sputnik.
We watched it one night
from outside our front door,
its silent elliptical low earth orbit
ghosting beneath Orion and the Pleiades.

We were astonished - no blue sachet.
The tang of each crisp
identical to all other crisps in the packet.
Truly a new world: brink of the age
of cheese and onion flavouring.

Christine

Below the Wesleyan chapel,
across from Smallwood's farm,
Charlie Soothill's chip shop.
Saw to the bets until it became legal
and someone opened a bookie's.
Spent each-way pennies
down The Travellers on a Saturday
after he'd cleaned the green range,
Frank Ford Halifax across the top.

Best batter in the land.
Took a chip from each frying,
tested it between finger and thumb.
A look was enough for the fish.

In the window next door, Charlie's daughter.
Laughed when we offered a seasoned chip,
laughed at summer sunsets, snow,
dust blown down the street on darkening days.
We'd never heard the word *Downs*,
only two-syllabled insults
we couldn't call her. Christine,
always on the other side of the glass.

Neighbour
(i.m. Tony Wilson)

After the war he bred pigs
in the crumbling outbuildings of Crow Nest mansion
where unexpected crashings would shake
the silence of still summer nights
as three-hundred-million-year-old millstone grit
settled back into the grass.

Once he was a black-haired horseman
with an Errol Flynn moustache,
three-quarter in the rugby team,
hands in pockets in that focussed moment,
imagining, I imagine,
this will last for ever.

In the Burma jungle, late one afternoon,
while he lolled with a cigarette
beside a mound of foreign flowers
by a single track railway,
an air attack reduced his platoon to one.
He came home, horse bolted,
sweethearts metamorphosed and married,
not knowing his own mother.

When I helped for a day
we picked up feed at the flour mill,
filled the troughs with swill,
marvelled at the massive old boar
rising from the straw
like a great whale outgrowing its ocean,
bristles like a brush's on its back.

After thirty years he put on his coat,
let himself out, walked down the grounds,
scratched his hands on the brambles
as he climbed the embankment
and lay on the Ilkley line
in front of the evening train,
having, the papers said,
been depressed for some time.

World Tree

In a corner of Three Days Work
by a stile which takes the path
to the back of the old graveyard:
ash, shelter and shade
for beasts in summer.

You could stand on the coping
of the weather-mangled wall –
scrags of blackened sandstone –
pull yourself onto its lowest branch,
inch along rough ridges of bark
to its centre, climb

to where you would see
wheatfields over the embankment,
then lean and close your eyes,
listen to the breeze
as it brushed the leaves,
soft as love.

Lightning felled this one.
It lay for years, diminishing,
until someone saw to it
and emptiness filled the field.

Late Spring

The first snowdrops we saw
climbed the height of a steep bank.
We both remarked on its steepness,
saying it was a surprise
that such abundance could survive
in a setting so unwelcoming,
never mind their persistence,
year after year.

Then they were everywhere:
beside the beck, along the grassy edges
where the lane sloped up from the village,
beneath hedges of hawthorn, fences and walls,
in corners of gardens.
You wouldn't have thought the world
had been icy white for weeks
before yesterday's rain.

Enchanted plant plucked only by the gods,
flower white as milk,
antidote to Circe's poison,
cures the land of winter.

Friends Reunited

There you were, on a wooden bench
at the edge of the pitch,
long hair held back by a band,
hands linked in the lap
of your black school skirt,
toes just touching the grey grass
in this monochrome memory
of many-troubled long ago.

I remember one town-centre Saturday
in drizzle-dark December:
you in your yellow PVC raincoat
fashionably, I supposed, tied
at the waist, making your way
from the 41 bus
to where I lolled, combat-jacketed,
by the Gents in George Square.

Listening one afternoon, in your best room,
to records from the family collection,
with the approval of your mother:
Glen Miller, West Side Story;
words which should have felt
like unfolding April leaves
falling instead through empty air
to find a place for us nowhere.

And here you are, hardly called to mind
through half a century, seeming
more familiar now than then
as the perspective of decades
tapers to a yellow plastic topcoat
and an unasserted smile.
There's no time like the past.

Gambit

Mid-afternoon, the temperature
at Central Park Weather Station
a record one-hundred-and-four
in the shade at about the time,
burning beneath a blaze of borrowed eyes,
I trailed the littered streets of Greenwich Village
in search of something the changing times
had taken. (Better never than late?)

In a basement bistro on Bleecker Street
I shared a table with a woman of about my age,
from Dublin; before long she was telling me
she used to spend the winters in California,
summers in Massachusetts, that Prince Charles,
she had on authority, was gay. Touched
by her frankness, I imagined she had,
in the past, suffered for such loyalism.

Momentarily surprised by a noise
outside, we looked up to see a man
with blood across his face, a tale to tell.
With his tongue full of movie one-liners
he had high-nooned his attackers, winning
his wallet and realising, in late
middle-age, a leaning towards a kind
of wit. He asked if he might sit with us.
My friend told him she had well-wishers in
Wyoming, Andrew was the queen's bastard son.

Later, in Washington Square Park, I played
chess against a mid-westerner whose friends
were either drunks or dead.

                  We were watched
by a university professor who said
that much of his life had been spent puzzling
the nuances of this inscrutable game
and, briefly, two policemen, chewing gum,
guns hanging at their hips, heat everywhere.

No Matter

The shepherd said, *Ride on*
they'll part and let you through,
so I changed down a gear,
pedalled up the single-track road
past Greystoke Ghyll
just fast enough to balance
without whipping up a fluster,
and they did. Herdwicks
on their way to winter pasture
made for the verges
gave me a gangway,
and the sun shone low
over Great Mell Fell
on the amber leaves of autumn
and the shepherd smiled and waved
as I picked up my pace
in a following breeze
that late afternoon,
the thirty-first of October.

Honister

Where only Herdwicks had been, men delved
between hard grit bands and massive flags.
Closer the summit, better the slate.
Slid down by sledge, quarter ton a trip,
eight trips a day, all weathers, for splitting
and shaping in sheds, where late-starters
lace their boots, pack bags, make for Gable.

I jog down the grassy toll road to Seatoller
following, too late by centuries, Joe Clarke,
who once shifted five tons in a day. Behind us
Honister Crag, worked-out, takes the sun full-face.

One May Morning

I remember when they were
plastic-coated saplings, trespassers
on land that lived without them.

Now, thick waists of trunk,
branches like muscled thighs,
they define the land.

Ash, whose buds swell late,
slow-growing oak and beech
that root deep and live long.

Feathery larch, for fence posts
and failure, lanky silver birch
with leaves like tears.

In a clearing beyond holly, willow,
wrens' nests, when bluebells mirror
a spring sky, white figures

tread a Long Sword dance
to the tune of a village fiddler.

All the Same

There's probably nothing new
to say about blue June days:
rose-coloured clematis winding
around the remains of the cypress,
trimmed twenty years ago,
flock of long-tailed tits
trapezing on the bird-feeders,
jaunting across to the laurel hedge
and back,
elderflower leaning over the fence,
buds about to blossom,
garden chair on the grass,
coffee on the camping table,
then on my mind.
All the same, I'll say it.

Odd Man Out

Across the Tyne Tees watershed,
down the valley, heading south
beside the gathering strength of the river.
Lapwings tried their old trick
of feigning a broken wing,
call like the wheeze of a tenor sax,
as if I were a threat to nests and eggs.
A long time since I'd seen so many
and I laughed out loud more than once
at their antics, their needless attentions,
though how were they to know?

Time for five minutes
before tackling the next climb,
I settled myself on the toppled gatepost
of a weathered farmhouse,
looked back the way I'd come:
granite stile at the far side
of acres of wet grass, woods beyond,
hush of the morning everywhere

till the day was broken to bits
by a scream.
I scrambled round the ruin,
yowled something primeval,
stilled time for a tick
before the stoat ungripped its catch,
scuttered off behind a drystone wall.
The rabbit, moon-eyed, shivered an instant,
sagged and died on the edge of Holwick Fell
below High Force, teeming after days of rain.

Wanderer

He dreams of an early morning,
dew dancing like stars
in sun's low-angled light
along the beech wood,
blackbird song in the thorn hedge,
beck hurdling over granite rocks.

She stands on the hill,
hair the colour of elderflower,
dress of wild pink thyme,
with still words and red clover
unravels the thunderous nights
of his mind.

She is Queen Anne's Lace,
Sweet Cicely, blackthorn blossom
lighting an April meadow,
summer's wild strawberries,
blue-black fruit of juniper
on flaming autumn days.

Busker

Once a warm Cretaceous sea
covered this land, ebbing and flowing
around the island chain of Europe,
left behind patterns of flowering crinoids,
corals and sponges in Splash Point chalk,
foreshore of flints. She looked back
when all but out of sight,
started when she caught my eye.

Shorts, tee shirt, flip-flops
have survived the season.
Half-full of coins and sweets,
my cap crumples on the pavement.
I sing *Only Sixteen* for the last time,
calloused fingers picking patterns
on my worn acoustic, think about
the girl in the yellow dress.

Below me the bay curves
from jetty to bandstand;
beyond, on far-seeing days,
ships edge through Dover to Thames,
make for Humber and Dogger.
She lingered along the cliff-top path,
gave me a glance, turned
to gaze at the waves.

Tomorrow I'll roll up my bed,
take a train to somewhere
down the line, leave this place
to the weight of winter air,
dross of lonely driftwood
along the cold beach; summer
and the girl a half-forgotten song
no fossil hammer can reach.

Red Deer

Down from the hill
where snow drifts deep,
I round the last low drum.

Still as ice they stand,
Palaeolithic cave-painting
at December day's end.

A hundred or more,
sixteen-point antlers
a forest of bone.

Behind bulks Quinag,
massive white god
in a blazing blue sky.

I trespass along
the arrogant track.
Amber eyes fix on
my silent footfall.

Navvy

You've seen my embankments, cuttings,
tunnels where I blasted and hacked
through granite, Kentish coastal chalk,
millstone grit of northern dales.

With shovel, pick and barrow
I could shift twenty tons a day,
lay down the line where hills crowd,
rain soaks, and the curlew calls.

Packed in shanty towns, slept on boards,
bare-fist fights on gusty nights,
away on a randy till the money was gone
(lend you my girl for a gallon of ale).

Killed by winter, disease and drink,
killed by landslips, killed by the wind;
killed by capital's careless pace,
by honest labour's callous face.

Old Road

I

Straggling back from Adwalton Moor,
carrying wounds and the self-pity
of a home defeat, Fairfax's men

shelter from the browbeating sun
beside the track to Wynteredge
and the safety of Halifax.

Their leader, some way off, his horse
chomping at meadow stubble
left by the summer's first cutting,

rues the ruin of his battle plan:
Gifford should have advanced at four
that morning, didn't move till eight.

A soldier throws his pike
amongst the daisies and docks,
draws his sword, slashes a sapling

clean through its young stem,
sprawls among the wild oats
that have grown here a million years

or more, as an age's unfinished birdsong
is scattered from oak and ash,
barbed branches of thorn.

2

Hemmed in by hawthorn still,
Lees Lane is an exercise strip

for joggers and Labradors; the blackbird
has altered, by a semi-tone,

one note of its song, while lovers
with nowhere else pluck grey-haired

dandelions, lean back
against a massive bulk of trunk

blowing, into the restless air,
words, like dispersing seeds.

Home Guard

Their lean late-morning shadows
across the pitted tarmac of Leeds Road
and paving stones from Kirk Lane Quarry
marked a bright blue winter's day.

Top-to-toe in khaki that kept
weavers and dyers in wartime work,
they marched past bygone buildings and ginnels,
back of Smallwood's Farm.

Outside the Branch Library a woman
carrying a child and a letter,
wearing a coat two sizes too large,
paused at the post-box.

An old signpost by Barrett's Bakery
offered options at the crossroads.

Double Life

(*'I long to ride a bike, dance, whistle, look at the world,
feel young and know that I am free …'*
Diary of Anne Frank, 24 December 1943)

Summer again, she pedals beneath
Carrock Fell's volcanic crags,
tyre-rasp on dry tarmac,
gripping the camber round the road's curves,
spinning past low farms, limestone walls,
the Glenderamackin as it gallops
down to Wordsworth's Derwent
and on to the Irish Sea.

End of an afternoon, panniers strapped
over the back wheel of her *Ellis Briggs.*
Cranstackie heaves to the east,
its quartzite white in the sun.
She is the south wind
breezing along the strath,
winding past cairns and lochans
to the edge of the land, or

fourteen, freewheeling by Fleet Moss,
Langstrothdale and a lifetime before her,
glad at her gathering speed,
high-gearing through Hubberholme,
coming to rest by the bridge
in Kettlewell, where she thinks
she could lean and listen for ever
to the riff of the river's farewell.

The Cricketers at Keswick

On summer Saturdays they weave motifs across Fitz Park
between the River Greta and the pavilion boundary
where the ground swells to become Skiddaw.

Light on the wind and the eye,
in their mayblossom whiteness they seem like a newsreel
of something their grandfathers did in the thirties,
talking at tea of Larwood and Bradman, Verity and Voce,
or sitting beneath black drizzling crags waiting for play.

Norsemen came here, cleared the land of rocks
the last Ice Age left behind
so cattle could be kept, cricket can be played.
They passed the spot where Wordsworth would be born,
heard the water's ceaseless music,
settled where Coleridge couldn't.

Cricketers look up at close of day to see the same relief:
Latrigg, Lonscale, Carl Side, Dodd.
The sun loops through their lives in a faultless flight
over Derwentwater and Grisedale Pike
pitching, somewhere out of sight, onto the Solway.

They will wait all afternoon, weeks of weekends,
for the chance to become their quintessence.
The diving catch at deep extra cover,
the desperate second run to wide mid-on
that wins the match
is their vindication,
perfection in a perfect world,
as nothing else between birth and death can ever be.

Gathering

Back from the pit hills
along stretched-out fields
with a jugful of blackberries,
grandma's hand guiding me
through still-warm stiles,
down the snicket to her house,
weather vane at its gable.

In the fruit-stewed kitchen
they turned into pies and crumbles,
jars of jelly jam, or, strained
into bottles, bubbled for weeks,
became wine I was given a taste of
come Christmas.

Days without a stain, except
when she glanced at the framed photo
of the soldier in the hall.
Thought I wasn't watching.

My Father's Father

Just eighteen, first time abroad,
warmth of an Anatolian autumn.
Cruised home across the Med
on a hospital ship from Gallipoli
with a dodgy chest for life
until he died of it.

When we came for the afternoon,
went blagging down the pit hills,
he walked slowly through sunny fields,
leant on stone stiles gathering air,
looked beyond over blankets of barley
to Ferrills Wood and faraway farms.

In holiday photographs he wears
jacket and jumper, tie and trilby,
sits in a cliff-top deckchair
above crowded sands,
gazes through railings at the sea.

Close-fisted with words:
sentences short as breath
could check the click of knitting,
toy soldiers in the hearth.

Christmas Morning

Cold rain in an east wind
on grandad's allotment
where I wasn't allowed –
He likes to be on his own
when he's back from work –
except this once a year.

Icicle fingers ripping sprouts
from their stalks for dinner,
then into the frowsty shed
for his tale of the Territorials,
trained to fire a rifle, the time
they won the Bingham Trophy

when the town brass band
met them at the station,
marched them past a crowd
of neighbours and workmates
and folk they didn't know
along the High Street.

See the Conquering Hero Comes
in perfect four-part harmony,
cornets thrilling to the high notes.
August nineteen-twelve,
as hot a day as they'd known
the whole summer.

Six Kisses

Written in black ink in the local almanac
against the name of her husband-to-be,
against his regiment, his date of death,
and what was once his home address,

the slants of grandma's nib
on the thin paper weakening
in coherence as they cross
to the edge of the page.

If he'd lived, two generations later
my life would have never begun.
No black ink, imagined kisses;
her loss then, mine now, unsung.

Suitcase

Lifetimes later, back of a wardrobe
in a house for sale, beneath a pile
of old coats and hats, frocks from long ago.
Lifting the lid is forbidden intimacy,
undressing someone I'd never known.

Photographs of uniformed young men,
cottage in the country, a football team.
Letters to your angel, with all the love there is.
Postcard ('I am well') from the Dardanelles.
A flimsy off-white wedding veil.

Ancestry

Dad

I was at the old Kettlewell Youth Hostel
in the schoolroom at the corner of Park Rash.
We'd finished work Saturday dinner
and ridden straight out over Denholmegate
stopping just at the Winifred Café
on the bend before the Bradley turn-off.
I had a Holdsworth, green enamelled frame,
seventy-two inch fixed gear, Endrick wheels.
Eric Balmforth was there, Rogerson, Hank,
I've forgotten who else. Most weekends
Spen Valley Wheelers were up in the Dales.
You hardly met a car past Skipton then;
the odd tractor, a few cyclists, that's all.

We could hear the planes coming towards us,
following the River Aire, I suppose,
then turning back before we could see the lights.
They didn't need to be flying overhead
to sound close. Sunday morning at breakfast
it was on the wireless. That day we rode
round into Langstrothdale, over Fleet Moss
and Buttertubs, down Swaledale, West Tanfield,
stopped at Fountains Abbey, then home for tea.
A few weeks later, out one evening,
Eric and I cycled into town and joined up.
I never felt threatened in Kettlewell.

Mum

First house at The Albert that Saturday
was Robert Newton in 'Hell's Cargoes'.

The siren must have gone during the film,
but by then nobody paid much attention.

If planes were flying along the valley,
people used to say, from the engine sound,
"That's a German bomber," or, "One of ours,"
reckoning they could tell the difference.

Later – Molly persuaded us – we called
at the dance in the Oddfellows Hall.
I'd have been sixteen, and very shy;
I hardly danced at all, just stood and watched.

In my spare time I knitted balaclavas,
scarves and gloves in khaki wool from work.
I was in a reserved occupation
and always used to wish they'd call me up.

When we came back out – we didn't stop long –
there was a big glow up in the sky
over Bailiff Bridge way. We knew somewhere'd
been hit. It's a long, long time ago.

Coda

August evening, nineteen-forty:
unfledged parents bicycle and dance
while between them Bradford burns

and I, eight years unborn,
waiting for my call-up,
not sounding close at all.

45

St. Mary's, Kettlewell

It is Holy Week. I suspend unbelief
on a seat beside rough lumps
of lichen-crusted limestone, memorials
to unnamed lead miners, cotton weavers,
labourers on the land.

Above waves of slate roofs,
long-standing ash and oak, valley sides,
held together by drystone walls,
hang from Moor End Fell
like a line of green washing.

Glacier gone years ago, hiring fair,
Thursday corn market, mine and mill.
A notice by the tower says
the vicar leaves after Low Sunday.
Trippers and Swaledales stay.

Near the porch, the Norman font
with its boar's head carvings; identified dead
commemorated in coloured glass
alongside avenging and tender saints;
altar of English oak.

I stand outside by a brooding holly,
afternoon sun suddenly warm,
turn towards the lychgate,
head down to the river.

Waiting Room

With a flick of fins the fantails
twist and tumble, shimmy and climb
through clear water between shingle bed
and still air resting on the surface.
Hexagonal tank: perfunctory aquascape
of single black rock, more fit for a wall;
tall plant with a look of ivy,
and bubbles rising like hopes.

Our files are on the trolley outside Room A.
Have you seen to next week's nutrition?
Three rows of chairs; front left's mine.
I'm fitting things in, doing bits of both.
Opposite, a metal cabinet in battleship grey.
I'll get found out if they ask any questions.
CRE to DAV, DAW to DOD, DOH to DYS.
You just go blonde, you'll get there.

We're running late. There are whispers,
shufflings as bodies are rearranged,
timetables changed. The goldfish,
refracted in angles of glass,
wind and weave in their element,
while we, with a weather eye,
we sit on, stare at the floor:
blue linoleum, like a big sky.

The Beaten

1

In 1974, the year of the Three-Day Week,
a Hebridean incomer, weary of slugs and snails
making meal after meal of her blossoms and greens,
smuggled hedgehogs on to South Uist.

On the *machair*, beside meagre fields
with fractured walls, sparse crops of barley,
wild flowers glow like gemstones –
red and white clover, heath-spotted orchids,
gentian, daisies, purple vetch.

By the time the century turned, the illicit settlers had spread
beyond garden pests through the land of bent grass,
fed, so someone heard, on the eggs of protected birds.

Facing away from dunes and ocean
abandoned vans and pick-ups rust into the shellsand;
around them white-flowering Lady's Tresses,
harebells, eyebright and thyme.

After a one-sided trial
the fecund hedgehogs of the western isles
were sentenced to death by lethal injection,
commuted to transportation aboard a CalMac ferry,
back to where they belonged.

2

After ages of seeing it through,
the Gaelic-tongued quit their tumbling crofts,
names carved in stone in the last homes of *Cladh Hallan*,
stand on deck beside a stack of baskets,
watching the west until Our Lady of the Sorrows,
Beinn Mhor, sea pink and poppies, are lost
beneath the curve of the world.

Glass

It seemed to take
a time to fall
but I couldn't catch it
before it crashed
to the kitchen floor.

Five gone from
a set of six,
broken by accident
over more than
forty years,
though accidents
don't have to happen.

And the last glass?
Should we drink from it
or keep it stored
at the back
of the cupboard
out of sight?
Always in mind.

Likeness

Early September, warm afternoon,
leaves on the turn. A dry path
winds up through oak and ash.

On the ridge now and drifting north,
dwarf thorn and yew, limestone stacks,
my shadow rambling in front of me:

a darker self against blue moor-grass,
time smoothed to an outline that could –
shape of the head, slope of the shoulders –

be myself fifty years ago, vaulting the wall
at the end of the railway bridge
on my way to work in the quarry,

night after night catching the bus into town,
running up to bowl at weekends,
give of the turf beneath my studs.

No stiffness in the limbs, jolting of joints.
No hint that distances are clearly a blur.

No Direction Home

The job was beneath him;
more used to felling an old elm
leaning across a lane
or levelling a hawthorn hedge.

He wouldn't have noticed
the noise at the far wall
as his chainsaw scythed
the soft wood in seconds.

Now, on the concrete gatepost
next to raked-over emptiness,
a thrush, beyond song,
twitches from beak to tail,

each eye a bewildered world
hurled out of its orbit,
while the laurel,
with its nest and broken

blue eggs spilling their yolk,
is taken to the tip.

Mother's Day

I closed your door and turned the key
as if it were a trip to the Tea Rooms.
Gordon was tidying the garden.
The window-cleaner set his ladder
against the gable end,
said it was a grand morning.
You took out your purse,
paid them both.

We drove along the village
past the park with its war memorial,
built the year before you were born.
By the bus stop I took a left turn.
"Where are we going?" you wondered.
"Oh yes, I'd just forgotten."

They brought you a cup of tea,
called you by your first name.
On the television, with subtitles,
someone was trying to sell a house
with a pond and an orchard,
views across a valley to wooded hills.

You sat in the only armchair
still in your coat,
looking out of the window
at roof tiles, some sky.

December

These are the days of low sun
when light is splintered by
leafless trees in the larch wood.

Caught on the north wind,
from the topmost branches
rooks spill fitfully upwards.

Barton Hill is grey and still,
laid out above the lifeless dale.

The land tightens its fist,
waits for the solstice.

White-tailed Eagle

I cross the trackless *Parph*.
Behind me indifferent Atlantic waves
break along the length of Sandwood Bay,
with its red-haired mermaid,
its bearded sailor still knocking at night
on the windows of the broken bothy.
Beneath the dunes, shepherds say,
wrecks of longship and galleon
have been smothered for centuries.

Massive tussocks make for hard going.
I rest on my stick, face north
towards the oldest rocks there are
then nothing but cold seas
to the Pole and beyond.

Like a sheet of white shadow
close enough to disconcert
it climbs from the cottongrass,
iolaire sùil na grèine -
eagle of the sunlit eye -
smoulders for a moment,
still as a Stone Age carving,
until it rises, in its own time,
above this wilderness, the bay, the ocean,
leaves me at best
a fleck of a far-off star
whose gleam may never reach
this earth.

Notes and Acknowledgements

7   William Arthur Poucher (1891-1988), known as Walt, was a leading British mountain photographer. He was a research chemist in the perfume industry, taking leave of absence each year from Yardley, his employer, so that he could pursue his hobby.

34   The Battle of Adwalton Moor took place on 30th June 1643, a few miles from where I live. Fairfax's Parliamentarian force was outnumbered and defeated by the Duke of Newcastle's Royalists.

39   My paternal grandmother, born Ada Jagger. (We are related to Mick. The common ancestor was born in Morley in 1802.)

42   My maternal grandmother, born Ada Whiteley.

40   'blagging', more correctly 'blaggin'. Clifton, near Brighouse, dialect for blackberrying.

41   Bingham Trophy – Colonel Sir John E Bingham, a Sheffield politician and businessman, presented this trophy to the Yorkshire Volunteers for an annual competition in field firing. The Brighouse Echo of 7 June 1912 said it was 'the largest piece of sterling gold and silver plate ever manufactured in Sheffield'.

48   *machair* – low-lying coastal land formed by the deposition of sand and shell fragments by the wind.

49   *Cladh Hallan* – an archaeological site on South Uist in the Outer Hebrides, occupied from 2000 BC.

55   *Parph* – from the Old Norse *hvarth*, meaning 'turning'. Originally referred to the massive cliffs at Cape Wrath; now to its

100-square-mile hinterland wilderness. This was where the Vikings, who had sailed along the north coast of Scotland, 'turned' to the south. Hence, also, the county of 'Sutherland', their 'Southland', in the north-west of the Scottish mainland.

Particular thanks to Simon Zonenblick of Caterpillar Poetry, whose interest sowed the seed which became this collection. To Gaia Holmes: her *Igniting the Spark* workshops gave birth to a number of the poems. To the legendary and discerning Albert Poets of Huddersfield for invaluable advice at the weekly workshops. To my friends John Foggin, for his encouragement and example, and pupil-turned-teacher Tim Murgatroyd. Finally, to the supportive poetry community of Calderdale and Kirklees.